NICK CAMERON

The Little Book of Now

Copyright © 2021 by Nick Cameron

All rights reserved. No part of this publication may be reproduced, stored or transmitted in any form or by any means, electronic, mechanical, photocopying, recording, scanning, or otherwise without written permission from the publisher. It is illegal to copy this book, post it to a website, or distribute it by any other means without permission.

First edition

ISBN: 978-1-80049-657-6

Contents

Foreword		iv
1	The conditioned mind	1
2	Step into the now	9
3	Awareness	19
4	The veil of ego	27
5	Where do thoughts come from	36
6	Identification with thought	41
7	The power of the mind	47
8	Who are you	52
9	The many faces of negativity	57
10	Unnecessary suffering	62
11	What if	67
12	Challenging situations	72
13	Accepting of change	78
14	Flexibility	83
15	Fighting negative thoughts	89
16	Reactivity	95
17	Anchor in the present	99
18	The wilderness years	105
19	A life of now	110

Foreword

As you get older, something timeless remains unchanged.

It is something which isn't found in opinions, judgments or experiences nor is it found in jobs, relationships or health.

The only thing which doesn't come and go, is I. A sense of beingness that is deeper than thought or form.

Among other things this book will encourage you to discover your true self. Perhaps it will open doors within you which have yet to be opened. In many instances the doors have not even been discovered.

This book has invented nothing and will add nothing to you, instead it will help shed the mind made image of who you are, not through adding layers but by dissolving the noise around you. And in doing so present you with a self which is far deeper than a fleeting acknowledgment of I.

Included are short stories and real life examples to invite a truer dimension to the teachings, along with points of guidance and obstacle awareness, all of which are conceptualised in the form of written language. Though as you will discover, the true essence of many teachings arise out of the absence of need for words or actions.

You will frequently see this symbol ⨏ which allows you to take a moment away from reading and asks you to look within yourself. Take time with the words of the book as if you were watching a sunset: the next moment may not give as much as the present moment.

You may find the greatest benefits arise from taking your time absorbing the text little by little and not reading from cover to cover in one sitting. If you find a particular passage resonates, immerse yourself in it and sense the aliveness within yourself.

All that you are and all that you ever need is already within.

It is time to discover your true self.

1

The conditioned mind

From the moment you take your first breath as a newborn, the slate is no longer blank. That is, the conditioning of the mind has started.

Your most primitive learning strategy has been deployed and it must quickly identify what will provide the most basic survival needs. In only a short matter of time the simplicity of the mind transcends to one of immense complexity.

As more time passes and with greater life experience the conditioned mind becomes your blueprint for life. The development of likes, dislikes, opinions, judgements, threats and pleasures become established. Every decision when made on an unconscious level is actioned by the conditioned mind: it chooses for you, so you don't have to. You think therefore you are, or as philosopher Descartes said,

"I think, therefore I am".

The essence of the quote in its most literal form may resonate with many humans: the idea that you are a product of thought and your thought is something to identify in or you find yourself in thinking.

And therein lies a most problematic misunderstanding of the relationship between I and the conditioning of the mind. The attachment to thinking as an identification of who I am, paves the way for immense suffering.

In the same way the intricacies of a river have been shaped by its own life history, the thoughts and emotions which you may recognise as being who you are have also been carved by the past.

Without the accumulation of the past, who are you?

Imagine a life where your experiences would have been totally different. Perhaps if you were born into an Amazonian tribe or a country of different culture or religion. Many of the things which you today perceive to be who you are would likely also be very different. Perhaps that self would be totally unrecognisable to who you are today.

If the person who you identify as yourself is so changeable and is so much a product of past experiences, the question remains

is that really you?

Or have you become a product of your own conditioned mind, to a point where the mind made narrative has swamped any other recognition of who you truly are?

For many, this is true and they may unknowingly invest their life into complying with this false sense of self without identifying the greater depth of who they truly are.

In the absence of this realisation, the conditioned mind continues to set boundaries to your thought, actions and very existence. These unwritten rules can be represented by the kind of filter we put on a social media picture, or even a window veil. It changes your outlook and your perception: life is experienced, but only through the veil of conditioning.

Every person who is struggling with thoughts or actions is at the mercy of the conditioned mind. You may have experienced overwhelming emotions yourself. When this happens you have temporarily become totally identified with mind activity and the conditioned mind dictates your perception, or misperception, in that moment. The worry or fear which the mind projects may seem so real and powerful that you become a slave to the requests, either through repetitive thinking or destructive behaviour.

> *The conditioned mind has a gravitational pull, drawing you in and fooling you into believing you have to act upon it or some great consequence will follow.*

If you have ever tried to stop thinking a specific thought, you may have sensed a reluctance to do so. Not on a conscious level, but something is drawing you back to the thought. This will be explored in later chapters, but for now, know that in most instances when a problematic thought is not engaged with there will likely be no consequence, and the space once occupied by incessant thinking will dissolve.

You may have once walked in unfamiliar surroundings in the countryside. Imagine a scenario where you had to track your journey back to the start point without any device to assist.

Attempting to retrace your route after completing the route only once may prove to be extremely difficult as your footprints would be barely visible.

After the 10th time, things get a little easier, perhaps some of the grass has been crumpled and leaves have been pressed deep into the ground.

By the 100th time, your footprints have produced a new walkway altogether: they are deeply ingrained in the landscape and it makes retracing a very simple task.

The comparison here is when you practice a certain thought or action numerous times, the conditioned mind becomes an expert in reproducing it. You no longer have to consciously think instead you are drawn to it and it just happens. This is how we learn, both good and bad, but suffering arises when you no longer have an element of choice in deciding whether to follow a thought or not. When there is no choice you are at the mercy of the conditioned mind.

If you have attempted to stop negative thinking or break a certain habit you have already demonstrated awareness. In this context I refer to awareness as being conscious of thinking and thought patterns. This means you are likely to have a sense that something is not going right, something is problematic or life is not fulfilling for whatever reason.

Awareness isn't the total solution to the problem, but it presents you with an element of choice.

You can now choose whether to follow the thought, or to disengage. Even if you are not yet able to disengage, having awareness on its own is the foundation from which you learn to disengage. Often awareness may arrive at a later time and not in the present moment. Perhaps an hour, day or week later.

With practice you will be able to shorten the time between the thought taking place and the awareness arising.

The point where change takes place is when you experience the conditioned thought and awareness is present at the same time. This enables you to recognise the thought as it develops in real time and you can now exercise an element of choice.

The conditioned mind will probably attempt to dissuade you and insist it won't work. I would suggest you temporarily ignore that and just try it. Trying to break free of a conditioned thought will likely be met with great resistance. This is because the mind has become conditioned to engaging with the thought and the thought expects your attention. There is a deeper reluctance also: when identified with thought, the thought represents a part of your being.

When you try something different to what the mind expects,

feelings of alertness and conflict may arise. The unease which you may experience is the reluctance to comply with the conditioning of the mind.

∬

As you are attempting something different from what feels like normal, in the short term it can be helpful to be quite welcoming towards the feeling of discomfort. Like a new pair of shoes, at first it may not feel right. There may even be an overwhelming urge to put on your old pair of comfortable shoes. The conditioning of your mind will be producing an alert response to the new relaxed attitude: simply acknowledge that response and observe it.

> *No matter how much of a threat you perceive the thoughts to be, remember this: they cannot hurt you.*

The conditioned mind may continue to narrate hostility, insisting you are in danger. This is to be expected. The more you are exposed to this feeling the weaker the alert response becomes and eventually it will transcend to one of peace. The once alert response becomes desensitised and no longer craves the next thought or action. All that is left is an alert presence free from the bottomless stream of conditioned thinking.

> *Much of what humans think is quite literally nonsensical.*

Problems arise when thoughts are given the same level of

credence as rules are, such as don't touch the hot kettle because it will burn and don't drive at the red traffic light. It is easy to see how seductive thinking can be when thoughts are misperceived as vital pieces of information.

You become aware, then you chose to disengage with the conditioned mind.

When the conditioned thinking is no longer primary and you choose not to ruminate over thoughts from the past, or project yourself into a future moment, it leaves a peaceful void in its wake: the here and now, the present moment.

2

Step into the now

There is an ancient Chinese book of wisdom named the Dao De Jing which is a source of inspiration and enlightenment for many who have discovered its words. The very first chapter reads in part:

> *"being empty, see the wonder*
> *being present, see the appearance*
> *these two are the same but have different names*
> *this is mystery*
> *mystery upon mystery*
> *the doorway to wonder"*

The notion of living in the present moment underpins some modern therapies but has been practiced in spirituality for many years. There is a saying which implies

> *there is no fear or suffering in the present moment, as the present moment is a place where the false sense of self cannot manifest.*

Living in the present moment, the here and now, reduces mind activity to a place where pointless thinking ceases to exist. Perhaps more specific, the conditioned mind no longer dictates your life through various thoughts and actions when you are fully present.

In the area which you are sat now, find something to observe.

> *It could be a pen, or a flower, or a chair. I invite you to go further than a fleeting acknowledgement of its form. With an element of curiosity, discover everything you can about it. Its shape and depth of colour. Perhaps the subtle way light brings the object to life or the sound it would make if you were to interact with it. Do this without labelling, without narrating internally what you are seeing. For now, suspend the internal voice, as if there were no words for what you are experiencing: observe without thought.*

Perhaps you can already perceive in a state of alert presence without labelling, if so you are experiencing life in the present moment.

You may catch glimpses of presence at first or only become aware of presence once the mind has restarted its narrating and you have analysed the departed feeling of peace.

> *"Oh I wasn't thinking just then... and now I've just noticed I'm thinking again".*

At this point upon acknowledging the internal voice has become active once again, you can practice revisiting the present moment. The practice is to increase the duration of those glimpses of presence until they become primary and thinking becomes secondary.

What is the subject matter of your troublesome thoughts? Perhaps you replay stories rooted in the past, where you examine painful conflict or harbor negative thoughts over a stressful event. Alternatively, much of your thinking may predominantly be projecting into the future, into a time or situation shrouded by ambiguity, uncertainty and what if's. Perhaps its a mix.

To be fully present means you are no longer at the mercy from the incessant and destructive thinking produced by the conditioned mind, instead a healthy relationship with the tool of thinking is formed.

> *Would you leave the shower on after using it? No, you would switch it off. So when you have finished your productive thinking, you lay the tool of thinking to rest and continue life in the present moment.*

The present moment is all around you. Whether in a busy office environment or the top of a glacier mountain. You may be familiar with the saying "come to your senses": what you can hear, touch, smell, taste and feel is the essence of the present moment. When you are fully focused on your sensory input there is no space for thought to arise into.

There are steps you can take to become grounded in the present moment, which will be explored in later chapters, but for now direct your attention towards moments when you may have already been fully present in your lifetime.

ff

Consider the first time you witnessed a firework display. You were likely overwhelmed with excitement. The smell of bonfires, the laughing of older people. Being wrapped up in layers of clothing perhaps, in the UK at least. Singeing your fingers on the wrong end of a sparkler. And then of course the spectacle itself. The grandeur of the firework display, the shards of neon filling up the night sky, the bangs, the ooo's and aaa's from the onlooking crowd.

> *In that moment you were totally present, captivated by your senses.*

The conditioned mind was silent, at least for the most part. You were likely free from judgement as you were not comparing this firework display to the previous year, as you had not witnessed one before. You were probably free from labels because in that jaw dropping moment, there were no words or labels for what you were experiencing. The primary input was from your senses and thinking was secondary.

Fast forward into your adult life and you may have experienced something similar. Perhaps on a safari or admiring the view from the top of a hill. There were likely glimpses, minutes, where the noise of the conditioned mind was turned down, maybe to a point where you were free from thought and all which remained for that short time was a peaceful emptiness.

That moment was likely short lived before the incessant stream of thinking trickled into your consciousness and thought became primary once again.

You may have experienced post holiday blues, which is a stressful, even depressive state, upon returning home. On holiday you were likely present far more than in your typical day to day life and so when the holiday has ended, so did the sense of presence, and the discomfort of conditioned thinking returned.

Of course it isn't only pleasant experiences which ground you in the present moment. If you were to climb a treacherous mountain where one wrong foot placement would be fatal, or you were about to jump out of a plane at 15,000 ft, any feelings of guilt about the time you broke a vase 20 years ago would cease to exist.

In that moment you are free from conditioned thoughts.

Some might say they feel most alive in these death defying activities. The arousal and present moment anchoring of an extreme sport is unknowingly the very reason they are drawn to participate.

With practice, living in the present moment can be attained wherever you are.

If the notion of presence is new to you, consider allowing nature to lure you into the here and now. Walking in a forest, hiking a hill, relaxing in your garden or simply observing the stillness of a houseplant.

♫

A lady who came to see me on a weekly basis was finding it increasingly difficult to focus on day to day tasks. She was struggling to maintain any attention at work and when she came to relax she could not detach from thought. She was very much unaware that her life was being ruled by the constant stream of noise which her mind produced on a daily basis.

We conducted this particular session in a nearby park. This was quite significant as the story will illustrate. Upon giving her weekly update of significant events she went into further detail about her difficulty in focusing.

> *"I begin a task but I become sidetracked and pick up my phone, or I think of something else, or do something else."*

We spoke for a prolonged period on the present moment before I asked her,

> *"When you observe the park, tell me what you can see".*

She replied,

"Birds, trees, some people walking with winter coats on. I can hear cars on the road. ".

Next I asked her to pick one object and simply to observe it without adding labels or speaking. I wasn't expecting a vocal reply but she responded,

"I can see a parked car through the fencing. It has shiny wheels, sorry I'm not good with cars, it has a big exhaust and it's parked next to an apple tree which I also like".

She insisted that she understood the instruction but her reply just happened. A smile was shared. I asked her,

"This time imagine your eyes are detached from your body. Without a mind they have no ability to perceive, they simply observe without thought."

This time she glanced towards the car and her eyes became fixed. No words were spoken. After a short period I asked her to explain the experience. She immediately laughed and said,

"I have no idea what just happened. But it felt very strange. And quite boring!".

We explored what the label of boring represented and she described it as actually quite life giving: she felt free and alert. In effect she was experiencing alert presence.

Of course it wasn't long before the thinking mind became primary once again but the teaching was a success in that she caught a glimpse of an alternate state of consciousness. A far deeper one, which went beyond the conditioning of the mind.

It was quite a profound moment for this lady as she was able to observe the noise in her mind without engaging with it whilst also acknowledging that even in times of rest, her mind was never truly resting.

When you try this practice you are not entering a trance like state, more so a meaningful state: you are even more alert to life because your experience is not lost in commentary. It is life giving as it removes the noise of everything outside of the present moment.

∬

There are times when thinking into the past and projecting into the future is positive and even essential. When this benefits you it can be seen as clean thinking. What time is my train leaving tomorrow, when is the deadline for work and so on. But after using the tool of thinking, you can lay it to rest and return to the present moment. Even in moments which demand a period of consistent thinking you can still maintain presence as your anchor.

Being present doesn't render you unable to create assertive action or critical thought, more so, the actions and thoughts are developed from a deeper space, without egoic desire or fear attached to the decision making. You may have heard cliché stories of people from a creative background sighting,

"It just came to me"
"The song just wrote itself"
"The painting just happened"

Many creative people unknowingly access a deeper dimension of consciousness, away from the noise of egoic thought.

Ultimately the present moment is all we ever have. When the future arrives, it is the present moment. When we think about the past, we are doing so from the present moment.

When you are able to be fully present, the activity of the conditioned mind subsides with only short interludes of purposeful thinking. Something else takes the place and becomes primary: presence.

3

Awareness

You may have seen a person walking down the street talking to themselves and it almost seems as if they have been taken over or possessed. You may try to disguise your interest but there is a sense of curiosity about what you are witnessing. Like a tennis match his conversation goes back and forth amplifying and quieting in both noise and animation. As the man drifts off into the distance you may experience thought formations begin to develop such as,

> *"Thank God I'm not like that. Poor man, talking to himself, what a strange life to lead".*

And then a moment of awareness may arise when you realise you're just the same as the man, the only difference being you talk to the voice in your head and not answer it out loud. Most human beings think compulsively for much of their waking hours: there is an old saying, "talking to yourself is the first sign of madness" which is not to be taken literally but the essence is that being lost in thought is life denying.

If you talk out loud all of the time, you don't hear what anyone else has to say. When you think all the time you do not have anything to experience apart from thoughts, therefore you never gain a true relationship with reality nor experience the present moment in its totality.

The boundary between presence and awareness is intangible but without awareness there can be no sustained presence. Experiencing the dimension of awareness invites you to a state full of clarity which is not clouded by thinking. One could say this dimension is behind thoughts or it is the cinema screen from which thoughts are projected onto. By using awareness you become alert to the thoughts and thinking patterns which take you out of the present moment. Without awareness you remain imprisoned and at the mercy of conditioned thinking.

Awareness is a dimension of consciousness that transcends the thinking mind. You already possess awareness in its entirety, that is, it is in every human being and does not have to be learned. To achieve something you need time, but clearly with discovering something it is already there.

The label awareness is just that: a label, from which slightly different interpretations could be realised. I as the author may be able to give a conceptual understanding of awareness, but often experiencing the teaching itself will give more insight than words do, so allow me to give an example of where you may experience awareness.

> *When you listen to a presenter talking on the radio, she may finish a sentence and then there is a pause of a few seconds before she starts a new sentence. That pause which you are engaged with is awareness, an alert presence but without thought. You are conscious but that space is not*

populated by thinking.

Another example would be in speaking with someone you admire, or perhaps a motivational speaker, even watching a gripping TV show or YouTube video.

When you hang on every word which someone speaks, they may pause for a few seconds, but during which you are not thinking. There is just an alert presence, a stillness. You may experience the opposite happening when listening to somebody who you identify as boring: your awareness dissolves, the thinking mind becomes primary and you move away from presence.

The practice of awareness is an ancient concept. Even without religious belief the sentiment of this is still valid; the Buddha calls it emptiness, the teachings of Christianity would call it the kingdom of heaven or what is within you. In the modern World where thinking is glamourised, many humans have unconsciously traded awareness for thinking.

You may catch glimpses of this awareness more frequently than you realise. As with grounding in the present moment, developing awareness itself can be assisted by nature.

Perhaps when you get out of your car for a forest walk and you take your first few breaths whilst your eyes pan from the bottom to the top of a majestic tree. The branches are swaying, the birds are chirping. The scent of pine fills the air and you feel a gentle breeze against your skin.

For those first few seconds you are completely present, in a state of alert awareness. Your senses are painting the picture for you. Without sustained awareness the thinking mind returns quickly, and the internal story telling generates momentum. Have you ever tried to watch your favourite TV program whilst somebody attempts to engage you in a constant conversation? You may still observe the essence of your program but it is not possible to give both the program and the person your fullest attention.

> *Now assume the somebody attempting to engage you is infact your internal voice.*

It is easy to see how, in the absence of awareness, life can't be experienced in all its totality.

ʃʃ

When you are trapped in the thinking mind the moments of awareness are very short lived and you become surrounded by conceptual thought. There is of course great use to conceptual thinking: humans have evolved over thousands of years to develop this incredible tool. Thinking itself is not problematic but conflict arises when you lose yourself in it, or you become 'lost in thought'. As such it is understandable that many humans derive a sense of identity from the limited movement of thought which they experience.

You may have experienced obsessive thoughts or thought

patterns which return time and time again. In this instance the mind becomes colonized by thoughts which take over the wholeness of your mind. Sometimes a single thought can be so powerful that the entire world of a person is viewed through the veil of that obsessive thought, almost as if that thought has all the answers and is all that the person will ever need in life. Even in recent human history there are countless examples of this happening on a National scale.

♫

The dimension of awareness is so important because from there you can observe what your mind is doing. It is the key to recognising dysfunctional thoughts or repetitive thought patterns.

As is frequently referenced in this book, with awareness comes the element of choice, in that you are no longer at the mercy of the conditioned mind.

As your awareness of mind activity grows the less you will become possessed by thinking. You are able to recognise hostile thoughts as they form in the moment and even before they form. Awareness enables you to intercept the thought at the first domino, instead of trying to disengage once the thought has gathered momentum and become amplified.

With awareness you still experience thought, viewpoints and judgement but thinking does not relentlessly invade your waking hours. You choose to think instead of your mind being overwhelmed by thought.

A practice is to become aware of how much of the thinking in your mind is not only unnecessary but is destructive to your health, wellbeing and happiness. By becoming alert and observing frequent thoughts you can recognise any pointless emotion when it arises. You may have experienced the mind taking you for a ride, jumping from one thought to the next, often over historical events or things which could happen in the future.

> *The reason why thoughts have an inviting lure is because in the absence of awareness thoughts are not voluntary: they happen to you.*

Awareness serves you in these situations because you become aware of the frequent thought patterns and thoughts themselves. With fearful thinking the mind becomes incredibly seductive and you feel an urge to listen to the story. You are misled into believing you must think about it now or something bad will follow.

> *With awareness you recognise it isn't happening now, probably won't happen and even if it does happen you will be able to deal with it when that moment arises.*

The problem can be resolved in the present moment, but it cannot be resolved in the mind, because in the mind the thoughts are part of a negatively charged fantasy. When the awareness arrives and you become familiar with its appearance it doesn't have to take the form of words, or your inner voice narrating your awareness. This is not necessary, though it may help in the early stages of awareness,

"I can feel that thought returning again and I know I don't have to follow it."

With consistency and after inviting awareness into your everyday life the slightly contrived narrative of awareness will transcend to a natural sense of awareness.

I, the author, am communicating with you, the reader, through written language because that is all we have to describe awareness but in doing so it becomes conceptualised. Language helps to point out obstacles which you may face with developing awareness, such as the lure of the conditioned mind drawing you to think, but awareness itself is not a concept: just an alert understanding without commentary of the activity within your mind.

You can identify awareness as the space behind thought or the space from where thought develops from.

See if you can notice the next time a thought of fear, complaint or negativity arises in your mind as quickly as you can. When this happens you will observe two things; the complaint itself, and awareness of the thought. It is quite a profound moment when you are able to witness both thinking, and awareness.

When this happens you are no longer the thinker, but the observer of thought through awareness.

4

The veil of ego

In Greek Mythology there was a Prince named Narcissus, a good looking and rich young man. The story says he was once walking by a stream, with many onlooking women all seeking his attention. He knelt down to drink and upon seeing his reflection in the water, he instantly fell in love. He did not love himself as such, more so the image of himself. He was so desperately identified with this love he could not bare to leave the stream, so he stayed, and in time became weaker until he finally perished. This, of course, gave us the term narcissism.

The traditional interpretation of ego may be seen as a misperception of self importance, even over confidence and arrogance. It is a trait that many don't wish to be seen to possess nor associated with. But when we search for greater depth we uncover more about what ego really is.

All humans have an ego which is closely related and largely dependent on the identification and perception of I.

Ego is a false, mind made, sense of self. Humans develop this illusory misperception of who I am at a very young age, as soon as they are old enough to identify with objects and even thoughts.

This is my toy car, I am John, this opinion is mine and so on.

You may have witnessed a child losing their favourite toy. In the moments after immense suffering and sadness prevails. The toy wasn't just an inanimate object, to them it was a part of who they are: It was mine, it belonged to me, it made me feel good about myself and so on. The toy had unconsciously strengthened their perceived sense of self, the ego. In contrast if the child were to have become bored or stopped playing with the toy out of choice, no suffering would be experienced. The I, ego, hasn't been hurt or damaged, instead the child likely has a new bigger, better toy, which it now identifies with. The ego manifests in the next object, superior to the previous, in this example.

In a similar way you may have witnessed an adult having their opinion belittled and immense frustration and perhaps anger follows. As above, the opinion was not just words it was a part of them: it was mine, I believe in it and it gives more depth to who I am as a person. A belittled opinion creates conflict with the the ego as it feels threatened because the ego itself only exists in identification and superiority.

I was visited by a client who told me,

> *"My thoughts are driving me insane".*

He could not live with his thinking mind anymore. We spoke about the thoughts which he recognised as being hostile and invasive. They were not the kind of thoughts you would choose to occupy your mind, which prompted me to ask,

> *"How sure are you they your thoughts?".*

His reaction was bordering on one of offence, as if he'd been the victim of a patronising question.

> *"Of course they are my thoughts. They are in my head!"*

He proclaimed. I asked him what it was he didn't like about his thoughts.

"Well I don't agree with them for a start. They crop up and they are irritating".

So I asked,

"If they are your thoughts why would you tell yourself something you don't agree with? Why would you purposefully irritate yourself?".

He replied,

"Well I can't control them, they just happen".

That was his moment of realisation. I watched each tense muscle in his face relax. He repeated,

"they just happen!".

Why this was such an important moment of awareness is because for the first time there was some flexibility over the thought ownership. He had discovered a theory that suggested not all thoughts were his. If they weren't his, there was no requirement to identify with them. Instead of being his thoughts, they were simply thoughts which he experienced.

Trying to appease the ego, or attempting to maintain an ego driven lifestyle long term, is problematic and inevitably creates internal conflict.

> *A dog held a juicy bone between its jaws as he crossed a bridge over a shallow river. He saw another dog on the other side of the river who he was keen to impress. When he looked downwards into the water from the bridge, he saw a third dog with what appeared to be an even bigger, juicier bone than his. He quickly jumped into the river to snatch the bigger bone, letting his go in the process, but realised the third dog was infact his own reflection, and so he ended up with nothing. His pursuit of wanting more than the other dog, and chasing an image of superiority, ended pretty badly for him.*

When you have more, can do more, or know more and your sense of worth is defined by that judgement, this is the ego. If you were to make comparisons with others and come out favorably, this is also ego.

> *The ego driven mindset is problematic because self worth and value are dependent on others being less able, knowing less or having less.*

It is not a satisfying basis for the long term, when you are no longer able to out-think, out perform or out possess someone else. When this inevitable time arrives, as above, suffering follows.

∬

Does this mean you should aim for less and be satisfied with a mediocre life? Of course not. There is nothing wrong with possessing expensive items, having vast knowledge or great abilities.

> *But for that to contribute to esteem and not ego, it arrives with the knowledge that you aren't forming your sense of worth in being superior.*

You can enjoy an enormous sense of worthiness and power but it is not comparative to others, and not more than. Confucius, the great Chinese philosopher once said,

> *"If a man has gifts as wonderful as the Duke of Zhou, yet is arrogant and mean, all the rest is of no account."*

Perhaps reflect without judgement over the things you buy, the places you visit, the stories you tell people and so on. It could be the car, handbag or watch that you buy. It could be a subject your friend doesn't know much about, but you take great satisfaction from telling them all about it. You may find that the reason isn't at all for the simple beauty of the material objects, or to be helpful on the subject matter. If you strip away layers you may uncover the true influencer of these actions which is often fed by the unconscious urge to conform with ego and to reinforce a desire to appear superior.

ʃʃ

The ego is a great obstacle in attempting to give up bad habits, behaviours or thinking patterns. After all, good or bad, they are 'mine'. It causes immense conflict with the ego which is reluctant to give up anything I, mine or myself. There is a sense of giving something up is giving away a part of myself - if I identify in it.

> *"I am a depressed person. It is who I've always been and always will be. I don't like myself"*

I had this exact line said to me. When I met this person, they were truly identified with that thought. More so the person was identified with their ego, the false sense of self. They believed the narrative, it belonged to them. There was great reluctance to part with that story because no matter how destructive it still represented I, albeit through the veil of ego. The person wasn't aware at the time of what a profound statement they had made, especially,

> *"I don't like myself".*

I asked,

> *"Who is the myself that the I doesn't like?".*

The person paused in silence for a few moments, and then an inquisitive smile arose.

We may perceive our mind as being one, but whenever we encounter this kind of statement we are experiencing an identification with our unconscious, conditioned thinking. There is the 'true I' which is found within values, what defines you as a human being, things which don't ever change with circumstance and things which aren't achievable or of material. And then there is myself, the identification with thoughts, perceptions, past experiences which give us this sense of self. Or 'myself'. This is quite an enlightened discovery which may arise when the true I is discovered in a moment of adversity. It frequently happens in times of complete despair and hopelessness that this realisation arises to the surface.

> *There is less room for conflict when you seek your true identity from the things which aren't changeable and which define you as a person.*

Alongside this when you experience a deeper awareness of thought and actions, you move away from conditioned thinking and the ego transcends toward life giving self esteem.

∬

A person with an egoic identify and a low self esteem came to me with various difficulties with the primary obstacle being she felt drawn towards drama. She acknowledged many of her choices and actions were inviting, even encouraging of both personal and situational drama. After some back and forth conversations she found the source of the drama. It was her unconscious desire to appease the ego.

> *Drama gave her opportunity for an opinion, to judge and to make comparisons. These viewpoints belonged to her and gave her a mispercieved definition of self.*

A part of her identity belonged in the various dramatic experiences. She even cited that she felt alive, and had a place of purpose, in these fleeting situations. This lead her to discover it was ego that thrived in these moments, not her true self.

ʃʃ

To be free from ego may seem like an overwhelmingly large task but when you are aware of your thoughts and actions in real time, you are no longer trapped by the unconscious need to appease the ego. This awareness of the thought, but not being a part of the thought anymore, is a great awakening.

Your own awakening out of ego may come suddenly or it may gradually dissolve in the light of your true self.

5

Where do thoughts come from

WHERE DO THOUGHTS COME FROM

The Buddha was asked this very question to which he replied,

> *"So you've been shot with an arrow, but before you remove it it seems like you need to know who shot it, where it came from and why would anybody do that to you? You want to examine this in more detail and find out the name, height and age of the archer. All of this takes priority and you use your time to find out everything you can about it before even removing the arrow?".*

This is quite a practical interpretation but the essence is true for suffering generated thinking: direct your attention to removing the problematic thought, not on it's origin or where it started. There may be practical scenarios where delving into the past may help, and be a necessary step, in resolving old pain but in a similar essence it is easy to become lost in the past without moving any closer to reducing suffering in the present moment.

Thought and thinking can be seen as both collective and individual. Perhaps you have experienced a different culture where a different language was spoken, different religions are practiced and different rules are adhered to. These originate in the collective mind that many in society will share: they are communal thoughts.

It is easy to imagine how different your belief system would be if you were raised in the Amazonian jungle, or how your moral compass would differ if you were, somehow, transported to a time where Viking raids and plunder was a part of life.

Along with collective thoughts you also develop your own individual thought which stem from your unconscious, conditioned beliefs. What about thought ownership? What determines whether a thought belong to you? If it happens in your head, is it yours?

If I were to ask you to think of a yellow submarine, and you think of it, is it your thought or just a projection of my mind? There is an unrecognised difference between your individual thoughts and the many foreign thoughts which are temporarily renting space in your mind.

When you experience a thought, who does it belong to? Many live with a mind full of thoughts which have taken possession of and pretends to be them, and they don't even know it.

♫

An assumption could be thoughts which you experience belong to you and therefore should be seen as valuable. A deeper assumption would be many of the thoughts which happen to you are simply a reflection, a literal mirror, of what your senses perceive. Many become so accepting of every thought that whatever the mind throws out they grasp it firmly and don't want to let go of it, even if it is destructive in nature.

Thoughts which stem from the conditioned mind imitate you, and can be very convincing: but they are not you.

There is a Zen story which follows two men arguing about a flag flapping in the wind.

"It's the wind that is really moving,"

stated the first one.

"No, it is the flag that is moving,"

said the second. A Zen master, who happened to be walking by, overheard the debate and calmly observed

"Neither the flag nor the wind is moving, it is the mind that moves."

The interpretation being the flag and the wind are simply happening: the only significant activity is in the mind.

♫

You may have noticed that certain thoughts return and some patterns become overwhelming and unavoidable. How much of the negative thinking which you encounter are old, repetitive thoughts? These thoughts only return because of the momentum of habit.

You see things not what they are, but as you are.

In essence you experience the World through your conditioned thoughts of your past. If you hold a conditioned thought that the World is being tough on you, your observations become selective and you can easily misperceive the reality of how tough the World is actually being on you. The realisation that thoughts are mind activity and they do not define you is a liberating discovery.

A common questions is,

> *"Why do I think things that are hurtful and make me feel sad?"*

Thoughts are negative and positively charged but with great consequence the conditioned mind, the ego, pulls you towards certain thought formations. This is where the common misperception happens where you may identify a certain thought as belonging to you.

> *"I'm thinking the thought, it's in my head, therefore it is mine"*

This is an understandable assumption, but it is a delusion. The perceived thought ownership is nothing more than an identification between the conditioned mind and a negatively charged thought form.

The true I transcends thought activity and the content of your mind. The great realisation is that thoughts happen to you and that identification with thought proves to be problematic.

6

Identification with thought

I imagine staring at the night sky on a clear night. Thousands of stars, each with slightly different characteristics to the next. Some big, some small. Some bright, some barely visible to the naked eye.

It would be an unusual notion to believe who you are as an individual is defined simply by how the stars appear, nor would you believe you possess a particular star. The bright star doesn't mean you are intelligent, and the dull star doesn't represent your personality. So when you observe the stars, you do not identify with them.

> *The randomness of the stars could be compared to your thoughts.*

Most thoughts which you experience are a byproduct of the conditioned mind and are without significant meaning. Thoughts happen to you in the same way breathing happens to you. So just like the stars, most thoughts which happen to you don't belong to you.

♫

Have you ever had a song run through your mind? Perhaps a catchy chorus or a beat. It may arise intermittently before dissolving again. There is no method or pattern to it's existence and it may quite randomly dis-and-re appear again. It may appear more frequently than you even realise as without awareness, the song can remain in the background, camouflaged by the abundance of other noise produced by the mind. It may only be when you hum the song, or sing it, or give further credence to the song that the incessant 'loop' becomes apparent.

If you're not playing the song, or choosing to think of the song but you can observe it, what or who is doing so?

This is a profound moment of realisation for anyone to experience. And also one of the first steps towards disidentifing with thinking and thought.

♫

The majority of thoughts which the conditioned mind invite you to follow are simply bits of information. It is easy to develop a habit of following the thoughts because of an unwritten misperception: if you don't, something catastrophic will follow. That is the conditioned belief.

When you engage with a certain thought regularly, or an action follows these thoughts, you reinforce them and give them far greater significance than they deserve. They can feel fixed and almost like rules. Many of these misperceived rules are created in childhood, where the mind is very much in its egoic stage in terms of learning what and who I am, what I like and dislike, what I possess and so on. During these impressionable years you may have been told various instructions, from a place of protection or safety, possibly from an elder or a teacher.

> *"Don't touch the hot pan or you will get burnt",*
> *"Wash your hands before eating or you will get sick",*
> *"Don't run on wet tiles or you will slip"*

and so on. These are constructive of course. Difficulties arise when the instructions are born from an internal place of anxiety or worry,

> *"Don't do a presentation or you will fail",*
> *"Avoid social situations as other people don't like you",*
> *"You are a depressed person and you always will be"*

and so on. When you unconsciously attach your sense of self to thoughts they become a part of your identity and thus hard to give up because they are a part of you, through the veil of ego. The boundary between the story I tell myself and the true I becomes increasingly hard to distinguish. In Zen they say,

> *"Don't seek the truth. Just cease to cherish opinions"*

which we interpret as let go of identification with thought and then who you are, beyond the mind, becomes primary.

♫

Immense freedom prevails when you are able to change your relationship with thinking. You are no longer imprisoned by new or conditioned thoughts.

When a train arrives at the station platform heading toward a random destination, you probably wouldn't step on it. You can witness and observe it, but there is no need to engage with it. Without any effort it will simply move on and fade into the distance.

Like many teachings this is something to be practiced and you may encounter great reluctance from the conditioned mind in allowing you to disengage. As before, I would advise you temporarily ignore the lure of old habits without force or aggression, but simply to passively accept that it may feel uncomfortable at first. You will be safe in the knowledge that this new approach is going to benefit you and contribute to a richer and more meaningful life.

It serves you to become totally aware of your thinking because you are able to not only identify repetitive thoughts and patterns, but you can also separate fact from fiction. A thought of,

"I am a nobody and my life is a joke"

is a debilitating story produced by the conditioned mind and limits you in taking the necessary action. It is a negatively charged self fulfilling prophecy. Whereas a factual thought of,

"I have five pounds in my bank account"

is empowering as you have the opportunity to act and resolve. You can use the tool of thinking to plan, and then you return to the presennt moment. Having the awareness of thought not only paves the way for disidentification with thinking but it also draws your attention to the relationship between your thoughts and emotions.

You are not the thought: you are the awareness behind the thought.

7

The power of the mind

The power of the mind. Perhaps this could be personified by the captain who survived over a Year at sea, stranded on an engineless boat with only rain water and a diet largely comprised of seaweed keeping him alive. A common definition for the power of the mind could be intelligence and the ability to solve problems. Some might say a high IQ test is a guideline to intelligence, others would say it is the untaught wisdom of a wise old person. But there is also room for a deeper dimension of true intelligence which transcends the ability to accumulate and analyse information.

∬

The mind can is the greatest tool available to every human being. And that is an interesting notion to explore: the mind as a tool.

Perhaps for yourself the mind tool is never really switched off. Instead it fluctuates in noise, similar to turning the volume dial on a radio, but it's still there in the background waiting to spring into action whenever it wishes to. The tool is never put down because there is great reluctance to do so. It may be a surprise to hear that the noise, thinking, is massively seductive. It would be fair to say thinking can is addictive.

> *The majority of thinking is ultimately fantasy and pure imagination. Many humans fail to recognise in they are suffering from an addiction to thinking.*

The mind is a tool and so there are benefits to operate it as such. In a similar way to the first time you hold a knife, you learn how it works, how best to operate it, how to hold it and how it may serve or harm you. So it is logical to spend time understanding your own mind machine.

Thinking is there to be used for a specific task, and when the task is complete, you can lay it down and return to the present moment. When you park outside your house, you switch the engine off and when you finish pouring a glass of water, you switch the tap off. So after you finish your constructive thinking, a state of non thinking should become primary. Thinking becomes secondary and your alert presence, living in the here and now, becomes primary.

How are you using your mind? Or is your mind using you?

For many humans it is like having immense wealth but not realising that they have the wealth, so they may as well not have it. I had a lady visit me who had been suffering with feelings of depression for over 40 years. She had experienced situations of trauma in her childhood and spent a large part of her adult life casting her mind into the past and reliving those painful episodes.

"How can I let go of these thoughts?"

was a common sentiment which arose. The more we spoke, the more she witnessed how imprisoned by thought she had become. The thoughts which she experienced were old thoughts, they were the same thoughts she had as a young teenager. This was quite a discovery for her to make. I asked her,

"Do those thoughts serve you? Or do you serve the thoughts".

She realised that the only thing keeping the thoughts going was the momentum of her conditioned mind, like a record stuck on a loop. It was a habit, feeding off the wrong assumption that pain was in the present moment, the here and now. It was old pain. The lady came to me seeking freedom from her imprisonment without realising for 40 years she had been holding the key.

Are you suffering from life today or from a memory of the past? Are you suffering from life today or from imagining into the future?

Much of human suffering is born out of a past or future moment.

♫

If when you were a young adult you had been visited by a God or supernatural like figure who told you they will grant you a wish of intelligence. All you have to do is say if you want a sharp intelligence or a blunt intelligence.

Which would you choose?

Most would prefer a sharp intelligence. The pitfall is of course having intelligence but not truly knowing how to use it. As above, using a sharp knife without knowledge of how it works will likely cause great harm. The human mind has evolved to be an incredibly sharp machine but it is easy to move through life without reading the instruction manual of how it works and understanding the deeper dimension of consciousness which transcends thinking.

Out of the noise and into the life.

∬

Perhaps now is the time to take a retreat from the conditioning of the mind and discover the true power of the mind: who you are beneath the commentary of the mind made self.

8

Who are you

WHO ARE YOU

Towards the end of the Wizard of Oz, Dorothy along with the Cowardly lion, Scarecrow and Tin man make an attempt to visit the great Oz himself. If you have seen the film you may recall the group reaching the hallway within Emerald City and after just a few steps being greeted by an aggressive voice calling them to,

"Come forward".

They sheepishly make their way to the room where the wizard appears to reside.

"I am Oz, the great and powerful. Who are you?"

a green hologram projection of a mans face calls down. He repeats,

"Who are you?"

They each begin to explain who they are, before Toto, Dorothy's loyal pet dog runs to the side of the auditorium and drags a curtain back in his teeth, revealing what appears to be a placid elderly gentlemen. The man is stood speaking into a microphone whilst pressing gadgets and pulling levers to control the fireball and smoke theatrics which the visitors were observing.

"Pay no attention to the man behind the curtain"

the voice bellowed. But of course, the mystery of the man was blown. The great and powerful Oz was infact a frail and charming old man. He somewhat ashamedly introduced himself as the Wizard, but far from the magical and intimidating image he had been portraying.

The conditioned mind, and the image it likes to portray is identical to that of Oz: it is a false sense of self. It will present you with a mind made sketch of who you are and in many instances it is believed.

> *This is not your true self, this is a self which the ego has found identification in.*

By this chapter of the book you may already have greater flexibility around the perception of who you truly are. Even if nothing radical has changed, there is a starting point and room for flexibility, or an alternative to what you have assumed always has been I. Up until now your conditioned mind has presented you with theory A. This is who you are, and you have somewhat agreed to this albeit on an unconscious level. But now we present a theory B. It is a bold leap to detach from the ego devised sense of self, but an ultimately rewarding step to take. Perhaps your curiosity will propel you to explore further what lies beneath in the deeper dimension of I.

> *Without your past conditioning and without projecting into a future what if scenario, who are you? Without the labels, without your name, your likes and dislikes, who is the human being reading this very sentence?*

As we already know, the conditioning and memories are not you. They have simply happened to the true I.

When your pet looks lovingly into your eyes, or a newborn baby smiles at you, who are they seeing? It is beyond their comprehension to conceptualise your past and to pass judgement on your conditioned self. Instead, they see the true I: the essence of your very being.

∬

The story teller in your mind doesn't want to be silenced. Like a hungry child it may create more noise in order to receive the attention it feeds upon, but through exercising awareness, you do not have to feed it.

> *What remains is consciousness, the very bare fact that I am.*

Something far deeper is realised and you can see within yourself that there is something behind the thinking and the veil of the self made mind. You no longer need to devise your sense of identity from your past, it is still there if you need it, but who you are is far deeper than your personal history and the story of your life.

> *Who are you?*

There is no conceptual answer to that question as that would just be another thought, but more so you experience a direct realisation that there is more to you than thinking. In realising this you are not adding a layer and you do not have to learn anything new. You are simply discovering what is already there, the true self behind the years of self generated noise.

♫

The World which we live in gives way to noise, both literal and metaphorical, and it is understandable to lose track of your formless and concept-less identity. As above, if you have a pet, or any life experience with an animal, understand the self which they see is likely unrecognizable to the self which you perceive yourself as.

> *They do not see the egoistic self but a much simpler version, and a much truer version.*

I invite you to discover some kind of aliveness or presence that is separate from your memories or the mind made story. As your mind moves away from conceptualised thought you will encounter a dimension of consciousness far deeper than your background, your story and opinions.

9

The many faces of negativity

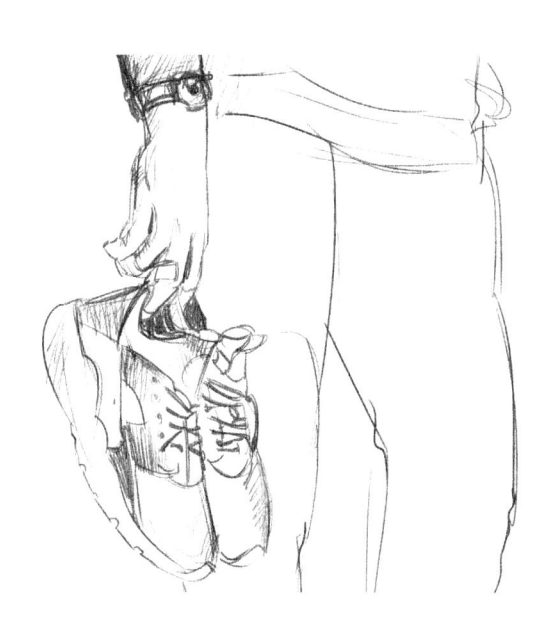

Many years ago when trainers first became a fashion commodity, teams of researchers were sent all over the world identifying potential new markets. Two researchers returned from a developing country to report their findings to the headquarters. The first researcher said,

"There is no market here. Nobody wears shoes".

The second researcher said,

"There is a huge market here. Nobody wears shoes".

When you experience negativity, what is it? Is it self generated, from the conditioned mind? Or perhaps it is witnessed externally.

If you could illustrate it, what would it look like?

One person who came to speak to me described the feeling as an angry beast similar to the creature in the film 'Alien', which contained row upon row of razor sharp teeth drooling with saliva, almost waiting for the victim to put a foot wrong. Another person had compared the feeling to a very plain, rusting, metal girder that simply swung whilst levitated a few feet off the ground.

Up until that point neither person had ever given an image to this feeling.

This is quite a significant step as in doing so they are observing the negativity as something other than themselves. They have immediately weakened the connection between the negativity and the identification with it. The process of disidentification has begun.

> *Have a look inside yourself. Ask various questions with curiosity. What is it? Where in your body does it live, or where does it develop from? What does it feel like? You can even go as far as describing it. Is it friendly, is it evil? Is it soft, jagged, does it resemble a cartoon or creature? And so on.*

You may have attempted to stop thinking a certain thought, or stop reenacting a destructive behaviour. There can be great reluctance to do so, even when you recognise it as a negative entity. As we spoke about previously the identification, good or bad, still represents I, the egoistic self. Perhaps you have lived with a negative thought for so long, you have merged and become one. You may have even forgotten what the true I feels like.

> *There is something within you that doesn't want to let go of negative thinking. It may be out of habit, or fear, or an overwhelming ego.*

The most important starting point in reducing negative thinking is awareness so that you are able to witness what your mind is doing as it happens, during a period of negativity. Though not as obvious you may also notice there is reluctance to dismiss the negativity: something is keeping you engaged. Perhaps you have witnessed somebody during a moment of anger and you may have asked them to "calm down". The person may become even more angry as a result: during that moment they do not want to leave the state of anger because the ego has temporarily been inflated.

Negative emotions will surface in different forms. Anxiety may be more subtle and gradually build or remain elevated for large periods of time, whereas anger is often experienced suddenly in short lived episodes.

If you have ever stepped on an upturned plug or a piece of lego you may have noticed that with almost no warning there is a reaction within you of immense distress or anger. I say almost because anger does not arise in the absolute instant. You may only have a few seconds to intercept anger before it fully develops, but with awareness you can observe anger as it arises, giving you the element of choice to disengage.

Without the early awareness, anger will build until the trigger has subdued or awareness develops at a later moment.

As your development of awareness in the moment grows so will the awareness of your emotional state grow. You may even begin to identify that certain emotions are old, learned emotions which no longer serve you.

An example being the present moment lure of arguing with your partner until you are satisfied with the outcome is comparable to when you were a child and arguing with a parent until you received the toy you desired. On an unconscious level arguing and attention served you.

These life lessons commonly go unnoticed as you progress into adulthood where without awareness they may still be routinely practiced. There is an unconscious belief that things will change if you are very unhappy. In the context of the child, this may well be true. The parent may on occasion give in to the screaming and give the child the toy. When this is practiced in adulthood the person often suffers because what was learned as a child no longer works.

> *It is the voice in your head which causes a large part of unhappiness and determines to what extent the impact of negativity becomes.*

Without awareness some people can live with this voice and take instruction from it all their life. They believe the mind made stories of "How bad my life is" and become identified with it, making it difficult to give up. Becoming aware of the internal narrative presents you with the opportunity to detach from unhelpful negative thinking patterns.

10

Unnecessary suffering

Much of the pain and suffering humans experience is born from fighting with what is. Without the knowing, or wisdom, it is easy to cling to fleeting moments as if they were permanent and everlasting. There is a quote which reads,

> *"No man has ever stepped foot in the same river twice, for he is not the same man, and it is not the same river"*

which encapsulates this essence perfectly and highlights the impermanence of both mankind and nature.

There may be moments in your life when you have 'put it off' or 'not thought about it'. You know it needs to be said or done, or perhaps a troublesome situation is on the horizon but you choose to delay action until there is no other option. There are times when you may wish you could change the ending of the story. Then when the inevitable arrives, in the absence of acceptance or acknowledgment, suffering prevails.

> *Consequently the mind feels unprepared and unequipped for dealing with the challenge of adversity.*

The fleeting nature of our existence is an unavoidable aspect of reality, so it serves humans to acknowledge and to accept what is. Resonating with this way of thinking changes the whole landscape for the problematic situations of life.

Perhaps you have been separated from a loved one, or your physical body has failed you. Your boss was unfair or your parent became unwell. Where did the suffering come from? Was it the situation itself, or how your mind reacted which caused the suffering?

> *"I wish i could switch my mind off"*

is a common complaint. But does your mind know any better? How can the mind remain positive when there is conflict between what is a reality of life and what your mind has so far learned to accept.

There may be times when you become entangled in drama, or on the receiving end of abuse and hate. This is an example of unnecessary suffering. Like a gravitational pull, it is easy to become part of the negative energy which does not belong to you. So why be a part of it?

There is a story where the Buddha was teaching a small group and a stranger walked past venting his rage. The Buddha said to the group and the angry man,

> *"If someone gives a gift to another person, who then chooses to decline it, tell me, who would then own the gift? The giver or the person who refuses to accept the gift?"*

> *"The giver"*

said the group after a little thought.

> "Any fool can see that"

added the angry stranger. The Buddha replied,

> "Then it follows, does it not, by our personal response to the abuse from another, we can choose who owns and keeps the bad feelings."

∬

We know that much of suffering is born internally from our misperception of events and thoughts. I'd like to reference a person who came to see me, who felt trapped by his own mind. He suffered from tortuous bouts of insomnia, and with every sleepless night, the pressure to sleep tremendously grew. After sometime working together he one day felt an immense sense of relief from the conditioning of his mind and he told me,

> "I feel like I've finally been given permission to not think these things".

The permission was not a literal grant of freedom but he had become aware to the fact that he was no longer answerable to the voice in his mind. He had grown up with the voice, it was as much a part of him as his physical body. But over the years he had become a slave to the voice and feared it's commands.

> "You won't sleep tonight"

"You've got yourself to blame"

were common thought patterns. He identified that this way of thinking was not serving him, instead he was serving the thought and taking instruction from it, in a master to slave like fashion.

Who was the slave? He was.
Who was the slave master? He was.
Where was the suffering coming from? Himself.

This was his awakening from which the relationship with thinking changed. He realised the fear attached to the voice in his head was perceived and it could not hurt him.

Over time he gave less credence to the voice and in return the hostility of the inner voice gradually dissolved.

Many times this book points towards the power of the mind in any given situation and that what you perceive or misperceive influences your suffering. So what happens when you give that privilege to someone else? You become involved in the ultimate slavery where someone else can decide your emotional state. As the Buddha said,

"Holding onto anger is like drinking poison and expecting the other person to die."

11

What if

It was the Dalai Lama who proclaimed,

> *"If a problem is fixable, if a situation is such that you can do something about it, then there is no need to worry. If it's not fixable, then there is no help in worrying. There is no benefit in worrying whatsoever."*

∬

The opportunity for fearful thinking gathers momentum when you project your thinking into the uncertainty of the future. By it's very definition the future is changeable and unpredictable and knowing does not exist there. You may have experienced what if thoughts yourself, perhaps on a minor or major scale.

> *"What if my job interview goes badly?"*
> *"What if my partner grows bored of me?"*
> *"What if I crash my car?"*

and so on. When the mind unconsciously attaches negative emotions to the what if, the what if becomes negatively charged. It is now not just a statement of uncertainty, but one carrying the weight emotion, fear, also. This makes the impact deeper and the significance greater. To explain further, there would probably not be any worry attached to an example of,

> *"What if I don't win the lottery this weekend?"*

It is quite harmless because it isn't negatively charged despite being born out of uncertainty. In the example of a job interview in two weeks time, if you were to listen to your mind, so much could go wrong and threaten your livelihood.

"What if I don't get the job, I won't be able to pay my mortgage, I won't be able to eat, I'll lose my home, my family might even disown me"

and so on. At this point you are engaging with and amplifying your conditioned mind. You are no longer experiencing a negative thought because a metaphorical struggle switch has been flicked on. What was once anxiety can quickly become sadness about the anxiety, then depression because of sadness, then guilt because of depression and so on.

Whenever you project yourself into a future moment you are entering a space of fantasy and imagination.

The conditioned mind tells you it is real, but this is a delusion of the mind. You may have noticed when experiencing what if thoughts there is very rarely a satisfying outcome. It would be unusual to be staring at a ceiling at 3am after hours of thinking and a conclusion of "I feel so much better" is reached. Instead, like a record stuck on a loop, the mind ruminates, trying to solve the self made puzzle but with many missing pieces.

It is important to remember the situation probably isn't as catastrophic as your conditioned mind is telling you.

Try it yourself. The next time you experience a what if, write down exactly what you fear about the pending situation, along with the likelihood of it happening, perhaps why it makes you feel this way and so on. You can go one step further and score the situation from 1-100 indicating how much you believe it is going to happen and why the result will be so painful. Note the repetitive thoughts which arise. After the situation has passed, reflect on what you wrote.

Of course the situation could be as bad as feared, in the same essence that a lottery ticket could be the winner. But more often than not this exercise will positively reinforce the conditioned mind was being too protective and your thoughts did not represent the reality of the pending situation. There is a moment of realisation which arises that suggests you were being misled by the conditioned mind and that it is safe to not engage with what if thoughts.

> *By not following what ifs you are changing the narrative from suffering to opportunity.*

You have an interview in two weeks time, but choose not to engage with any what if's as you acknowledge it won't bring you any closer to the interview outcome. It may even hinder your ability to be the true I on the day of the interview. Even if the interview doesn't go well, you can face the problem at that future moment, which will be experienced in the present moment, and take the necessary action at that point.

As with other unwelcome thoughts, what ifs can be addressed in a similar way. Through awareness and repeated exposure to what if scenarios, a belief will develop which reinforces what ifs do not serve you and they are not worthy of a fearful response.

The gravitational weight of what ifs amplifies only when fed the fuel of engagement. You may have noticed yourself, upon exterminating a worrying thought, you may immediately discover another. In this instance you are experiencing the momentum of the conditioned mind, which is suggesting to ignore troublesome thoughts would be irresponsible and that living a life of concern is serving you.

12

Challenging situations

You may be familiar with the story of a donkey who fell into a farmers well. The farmer briefly attempted a rescue but gave up as he thought the donkey was old and the well needed to be covered up anyway.

He began filling in the well with soil, despite hearing the donkeys cries for help. The farmer carried on and eventually no noise could be heard. A few minutes later, and to the shock of the farmer, the donkey hopped out of the well and trotted gracefully into the distance never to be seen again.

What the farmer didn't know was with every shovel of dirt he piled down the well, the donkey shook its coat, and took another step up, eventually bringing it to the surface.

ʃʃ

Human perception, or often misperception, of how a challenging situation is expected to materlialise forms the related actions and emotions. In day to day life we experience challenges from many sources. Perhaps a challenging job or a relationship or financial or environmental challenges.

> *If you are not able to change the situation, there is the option of considered acceptance.*

Accepting in this sense means you are at peace with, or welcoming of. You may not have to enjoy it but there is less room for internal resistance where negative energy can harbor.

Changing and accepting are the only logical solutions to a challenging situation.

Take note without judgement of the difference between the situation itself and what your mind says about the situation. You may see how the mind commentates and has a great role in how you cope with the challenge.

♪♪

You have likely experienced waiting in a shopping queue where perhaps the first few moments are without thought or emotion. But soon the commentary begins and, depending on your awareness in this moment, you notice a voice,

> *"This is just my luck. Why does this always happen to me? Typical."*

You listen to that voice, and agree of course, and it drip feeds you with more thoughts to fuel your reactivity. The longer the waiting goes on, the more you may become frustrated, stressed, even angry.

Imagine that same situation, but when the voice emerged, you detached from the story telling of the mind and you directed your attention to the present moment. You observed what was happening in the shop, perhaps you are drawn towards the stillness of a plant on the checkout desk.

When your attention is given fully to the present moment it is not possible for the story telling mind to be problematic.

In these situations you can welcome the challenge, offering no resistance to the fleeting nature of them. They will come and go. You may have to engage with some, but through your awareness, you can identify when not to become a part of the challenge itself.

I would like to share a particular Sufi story, which is neither intended to comfort nor imply fear. More so it gives an alternate perspective to the fragility of each moment and every challenging situation.

In this story there was a king who was either completely overwhelmed by happiness, or incredibly depressed with sadness at the events he experienced.

> *The king was at his wits' end. He couldn't live with his emotions swinging from one to the next. Nothing could bring him the peace which he desperately sought. He asked to speak to a local wise man, who was poor in materials, but said to be enlightened.*
>
> *The king relayed his story and the wise man offered a solution. He told the king that he could help, but the value is worth more than his entire kingdom, so the king must promise to honour the gift. The king gladly agreed. The wise man, accepting nothing in return, handed the king his gift. It was a modest sized wooden box which fit comfortably in the kings hand. The king opened the box*

and within it was a plain looking gold ring, but inscribed on it were the words "this too shall pass".

The wise man told the king that before labelling anything good or bad, he must touch the ring and read the inscription, that way he will be at peace.

Looking at this story literally it would seem these words are provided to give comfort in a bad situation, but they may also diminish the enjoyment of the good things in life. But there is a deeper sentiment which goes beyond that interpretation.

The inscribed words are making us aware of the fleetingness of every situation, because each moment is transient by definition. When we choose to invite those words into our life, we have acceptance, and are at peace with inevitable change.

Creating space between ourselves and unhelpful thoughts benefits us in challenging situations.

♫

Imagine yourself in a city centre traffic jam on a foggy day. Your windscreen wipers are sliding side to side, perhaps making a mechanical noise as they complete each motion. You see other drivers in their cars waving hand signals, some of which abusive in nature to other drivers. You can sense frustration and anger.

Now imagine yourself at the same city centre, but now you

are in a hot air balloon, 5000ft above the ground. The pandemonium is still happening beneath you but all you can observe is blue skies, above the fog, some distant snow capped mountains. You witness flocking birds dipping and diving beneath you. You sense aliveness and peace. The traffic jam is still happening but you have created space between yourself and the activity. These are quite a contrast in situations, but the sentiment remains:

The only thing that has really changed is your perception and that there is now space between you and thought.

The commentary which the mind is producing has transcended to an enjoyable one making the experience an end in itself, as opposed to a means to an end. Even without the contrast in viewpoint, your perspective can still give you a life giving experience.

13

Accepting of change

ACCEPTING OF CHANGE

There was a caterpillar, quite content with life, who became friends with a butterfly. The butterfly asked him,

"When you become a butterfly, where will you fly first?".

The caterpillar replied,

"I don't want to be a butterfly. I know who I am and I'm comfortable with who I am. Why do you want me to change? I belong on the ground, I don't want to be in the air."

No matter how much encouragement was given to the caterpillar, the butterfly had to wait until his friend was ready to change. The caterpillar went through immense suffering and continued to deny what was ultimately inevitable. He struggled with not being able to crawl and after days of becoming immobile he acquiesced to chance,

"I just can't take this anymore. I think I'd rather be a butterfly".

♫

You will likely have had years of developing your mind on an unconscious level. You have formed opinions and judgments. Perhaps you have worked for many years or studied at school or a University. You may have encountered times of financial security and then times of insecurity. You have possibly been in love or fallen out of love. Maybe you have had times of bad health but for the most part you have been healthy. Lots has happened, continues to happen and has changed.

In all that has changed, what has stayed the same?

♫

Is it your thoughts? No, your thoughts continue to change.

Is it your body? No, the cells of your body have been replaced.

Perhaps your job or various relationships? No, these have all changed over time.

The only constant in your life has been, and will continue to be I. The true I, your true self. The self which, with awareness, observes the conditioned self and all that changes with and around it.

It is easy to see why many humans chase the never ending dream of attempting to find who they are in change. Many look for fulfillment and a sense of worth in life's fleeting moments. It may come after years of relentless searching for ones self that the profound realisation emerges: the true I isn't found in external form, but it was always here, within.

This is why the concept of change can inflict so much dread, fear and reluctance to welcome it. When the sense of self is derived from a fleeting concept then change would understandably be a worrying and problematic reality to face.

∬

Change becomes easier to accept if an anchor is rooted in it. Greater acceptance of change can be realised when you are to acknowledge that all form is temporary, life itself is temporary. But that acceptance does not have to flood the mind with a sense of pending doom. With our great knowledge and ability to conceptualise comes an understanding of our fate. As soon as we are old enough to observe what happens to an apple left on a windowsill we may catch a glimpse of what will happen to us, someday.

It was the Buddha who said,

> *"Everything changes, nothing is without change".*

Change happens, but that is inevitable. The struggle which humans experience is not caused by change itself, but the misperception of what impact change will have. You may have identified this common viewpoint is one made through the veil of ego; I don't want my job, my car or life to change because my sense of self belongs in these things.

Have you ever tried to let go of something you have become attached to? Suffering likely prevails, in almost all cases, because you have an element of identity in the object, physical body or person and so on.

You might not even know you are identified with an object until it disappears. The feeling of attachment dissolves naturally, without effort, when there is no longer a sense of self found in the object.

14

Flexibility

The understanding of mental flexibility has been given ultimate importance throughout human history. There is a chapter in the Dao De Jing which figuratively talks about the importance of flexibility,

> *"People are born soft and weak*
> *They die hard and strong.*
> *All creatures, grass and trees are born soft and fragile,*
> *They die dry and withered.*
> *Hard and strong are disciples of death,*
> *Soft and weak are disciples of life.*
> *An unyielding army is defeated,*
> *An unbending tree is ready to fall.*
> *Big and strong dwell below,*
> *Soft and flexible dwell above."*

Some interpretations point us to believe the last profound insight refers to the structure of a tree, in that soft and yielding overcomes strong and hard. This may have given rise to the proverb "better bend than break" or "a tree which is unbendy is easily broken". A variant Greek version talks about an olive tree mocking a reed for being so submissive to every gust of wind. Of course when a terrible storm arrived and devastated all in its path, the reeds remained unscathed.

> *How much conflict is created by being fixed in your ways,*
> *both internally and externally?*

Flexibility, or lack of, could be seen as a relative of stubbornness. Not a trait which is viewed as a major character pitfall but it proves to be problematic. It is easy to see how if things don't go to plan at work, or the hotel room isn't what you expect, feelings of conflict and frustration has space to arise into.

Does this mean you accept the sub par hotel room? No. But your flexibility gives space to patience, understanding, that the situation will be resolved without the need for internal conflict.

We can see now how much of human suffering is self inflicted. Whether born out of ego, misperceptions or the relationship with thinking.

∫∫

I had a client who identified a lack of flexibility in her life. She was 'black and white' and because of previous bad experiences, had rigid views on men. More so, she was at the mercy of her conditioned mind and continued to take instruction from it.

She told me on numerous occasions quite enthusiastically that all men are the same, and unless a man is quiet and witty she will automatically dismiss any interaction with him either in work or in a relationship sense. This is a common viewpoint and is understandable when somebody is viewing life through the veil of conditioned thinking, ego. The lady had her trust and happiness broken and in similar essence to the child learning not to touch the hot kettle, she learnt to avoid situations where she could be hurt again.

What is more problematic is it worked: the conditioned

mind spared her from suffering.

So she continued for the next 8 years without any meaningful interaction with men and she encountered no conflict. But in doing so, had also closed the door on life giving, meaningful relationships with males. On the surface there is no problem with not wanting to engage with males: this was her prerogative. The reason why this was problematic is it had also presented her with a life denying way of dealing with conflict: avoidance.

In this instance her conditioned mind protected her but also greatly misled her into believing the 3 bad experiences she had experienced was a good reason to impose a life long ban on the other 3.7bn males out of a mind made fear of what if. There was no flexibility. She was rigid and would be protective of her viewpoint.

We spoke for many sessions and in time she brought balance into her life. Without being dismissive of important life experience her flexibility and awareness helped her form a judgment not born out of the conditioned mind, which was aligned to her values as a person and what would contribute to a rich and meaningful life.

Did she hate males? No, quite the contrary. She was a loving mother to her son and was a care worker for vulnerable young adults of both genders. She enjoyed male company, when on her terms. She was full of compassion and care. But the impact from previous experiences had shaped her mind and, when walk down the muddy path often enough, her minds footprints had becomes solid and inflexible.

Her profound moment arose when she realised this way of thinking was no longer serving her, instead she was serving it and she recognised why she experienced certain overwhelming feelings.

She figuratively removed the protective plaster and noticed the wound had healed; the pain was old pain, the emotions were no longer raw. That was when she awoke out of the self made boundaries.

∬

What do you perceive as being a normal emotional state in humans? You may experience moments of frustration or sadness when comparing to others and the mispercieved picture of their happiness. Those feelings may even amplify to ones of resentment and jealousy. This occurrence is ever present today with the influence of TV and social media. You can greatly reduce unnecessary suffering by considering the emotional state of humans is ever changing: ups and downs. If you are to take this literally there will be times of immense happiness and sadness.

In this instance you accept that emotions are changing and that flexibility with your emotional expectations will serve you.

You can use mental flexibility as a tool to help overcome various difficulties and challenges in life and to become comfortable with uncertainty, or the feeling of not knowing.

> *Ultimately when you are more flexible in the mind, you no longer expect perfection from an imperfect World.*

Being welcome to uncertainty reduces the level of conflict which you encounter, as you are now open to the unpredictability of life.

15

Fighting negative thoughts

There's a simple story about a frog who tried to reach the top of a tree. The canopy was some way up and it seemed like quite the distance for the frog to reach. Nevertheless he started its journey and half way up he could hear all the other frogs on the floor shouting.

The frogs on the ground were saying among themselves "it's impossible, give up, you can't do it". The frog continued and eventually reached the top. Upon returning to the ground he was thankful to the other frogs and said he couldn't have succeeded without their support.

We learn the frog was deaf and assumed the other frogs were shouting words of encouragement to him. The underlying teaching from this Buddha story is to be deaf to negative thinking if you want to reach your goal.

∬

It is human nature to fight negative thoughts or wrestle with adversity, more generally speaking. The essence of standing up to the school bully, or fighting fire with fire is a common practice. The quote attached to Winston Churchill holds a similar sentiment,

"When you're going through hell, keep going".

It is understandable that humans would also adopt this approach to internal battles.

FIGHTING NEGATIVE THOUGHTS

We know that fighting, more so engaging, with negative thoughts doesn't work. When you engage with a negative thought you are keeping an element of momentum going. A thought is a type of entity, not in a horror sense, but it is a small energy form. It feeds on attention, so whether the engagement is positive or negatively charged it still becomes more than before.

If you try hard not to think of a yellow mini for 30 seconds observe what happens.

You may be able to temporarily block out the yellow mini by forcing your mind elsewhere but that will soon subside once the distractions have dwindled and the thought of a yellow mini arises again. Even when you aren't thinking of the mini directly, somewhere in your consciousness you are aware that you are trying not to think of the yellow mini. So trying not to think, or diverting our attention, doesn't work either.

∬

What we know is these negatively charged thoughts can only perform if given a stage to perform on and you as the audience do not have to entertain the performance. You may have made some connections with previous chapters, in that, when you become conscious of thinking and aware of patterns an element of choice arises. In this instance you don't need to forcefully detach from a thought, but actually be welcoming of it. This could be seen as counter productive; why would you intentionally welcome a problematic or distressing thought?

The analogy of the grass is always greener on the other side springs to mind. Why do cows poke their heads through the tiniest of field fences to graze on the muddy roadside grass when the grass in the field is green and luscious? Why is there a certain lure and excitement towards something which is highly sought after, but you can't have? The mind works in a similar way with attention and thinking.

> *Deny it, it will want more. Give it more, it becomes disinterested . With regular exposure the once alert, exciting or fearful response transcends to one of boredom.*

It is important not to hone in on the label, or the words used, to describe our welcoming attitude to negative thinking. You may call it passive, offering no resistance, at peace with and so on. The label isn't important, more so the teaching is without label, it is the underlying sentiment that when a negative thought arises you allow it to wash over you without engagement.

♫

The weather can be a useful metaphor for our feelings and dealing with negative thinking. Firstly we understand that emotions, just like the weather, are very changeable and that all humans feel moments of happiness and sadness.

We also know that each storms passes, as does a sunny day, so we learn to value and accept them both. Your thoughts happen to you in the same way the weather happens to you. It would be an unusual notion to physically try and push the clouds away on an overcast day.

Many people have asked even pleaded,

> *"Help me get rid of these thoughts. I can't stop thinking them".*

Is the problem the thought, or what you choose to do with the thought? When a train arrives at the platform, not going to your planned destination, do you argue with the train and ask how can I stop it? The energy should be removed from the train and onto your element of choice which comes with awareness. You can choose to engage with the train or simply wait for your planned train.

♫

The Dalai Lama said,

> *"Silence is sometimes the best answer".*

We can interpret this both in a physical and mindful sense. A thought doesn't always need a reply and does not need to be fought with. The battle with negative thinking is won when you stop trying to battle with negative thoughts. This acceptance of negative thinking happens when you are living life in the here and now: so your practice can include living more presently because awareness transmutes fear into presence.

When you truly connected to the moment as awareness of fear instead of unconsciously identifying with fear, it naturally fades away and dissolves into a state of stillness.

16

Reactivity

One day a small field mouse awoke from his nest to find himself between the paws of a huge sleeping lion, which immediately awoke and seized the mouse. The mouse pleaded with the lion to be set free. The lion was old and wise, and in no need of such a small meal, lifted the mouse up with its paw and pushed it on its way.

A few days later in a nearby forest, a hunter had laid a trap which snared the lion. There he remained, swaying upside down helpless, with nothing to do than wait for the hunter to return and seal his doom.

Of course, the mouse passed by before the hunter, and seeing the lion in need of help, promptly set about biting and gnawing through the net, which soon began to unravel, setting the great lion free.

Similar to the lion, you may have experienced a situation in which you reacted, or overreacted, during a moment. A common afterthought is,

"Why did I choose to react that way?".

♪

Most often you don't consciously choose to react, as most are being driven by the unconscious, conditioned mind. The choice of reacting only becomes an option when we are aware and are able to master our own reactivity.

When people meditate, or even seek peace, they may choose a quiet room, or perhaps they may even visit a hill for sunset, or a morning at the beach. These would appear idealic and thus the best places to perform relaxation. This example focuses on meditation but the same comparison can be made to any moment of reactivity.

> *Imagine you are in a quiet room during a moment of relaxation or meditation. What happens when the neighbours dog starts barking, or children playfully scream, or drilling begins breaking up a road outside your window. The first few seconds you may convince yourself it is fine, and hope it stops. After a few more seconds your mind may present you with various thoughts such as "this is a waste of time", "I can't meditate under these conditions" and so on.*

But what is problematic about the situation? Is it the noise, or the reaction?

In this instance you would allow the noise to be present and use distractions as part of the meditation, or relaxation, itself. The narrative changes to one of great opportunity; the noise presents itself as a door to a deeper dimension of consciousness. It can help to incorporate seemingly annoying things in practice by not offering any resistance to the present moment.

> *It is the reaction which causes the suffering.*

If your happiness is determined by what happens around you then the opportunity for unhappy experiences grows. When you become nonreactive to a situation what happens within you is determined by you, and the emotions you experience are no longer at the mercy of what happens around you.

Before you can become nonreactive spend time observing what form the reactivity takes so that when the situation arises, you realise the most important thing here is your state of consciousness.

When you are conscious, in that you aware of your mind activity and not lost in thought, you will not react. In a moment of unconsciousness where you are heavily identified with thought, you will likely be pulled in to a reactive state.

Perhaps it is anger, irritation or frustration that provokes a reactive response within you. Using your awareness develop familiarity with the pre-reactivity feeling. That is, there are situations where you can almost see it coming: you have to be very alert in these moments where you can see that reactivity is beginning to take form. In the example of anger, you may sense the red mist arising or the rumbles of internal thunder forming. You are not trying to remove the triggers for your reactivity, which would be an impossible task, but instead use them as an opportunity to further develop your own depth of awareness and consciousness.

These triggers can be seen as a spiritual practice in that when they arise you are practicing awareness and becoming more conscious: therefore your emotional state is no longer a slave to the reactive situation.

17

Anchor in the present

On many occasions throughout this book I have referenced the present moment, the here and now.

Many unknowingly live by the conditioned belief that a future moment has more value than the present moment. The here and now becomes devalued and a future uncertain moment becomes prioritised.

As talked about previously, thinking into a future or past moment can serve a purpose so in these instances you can choose to engage in the tool of thinking. The suffering arises when a future moment is relentlessly chased and in doing so the totality of the present moment is sacrificed.

You may be familiar with cliche stories of people who 'made it' or became a 'success' and experience immense satisfaction but soon transcends to emptiness. In many instances the pursuit was masking a far deeper need, so dissatisfaction arrives when the success is no longer enough. They chase a future moment falsely believing it will deliver sustained fulfillment, but unknowingly they are being driven by the unconscious need to appease the ego.

When you look for fulfillment in the present, it becomes an end in itself, rather than a means to an end. The small things in the here and now become valued when the mind is not caught up in chasing the future moment, which is never even experienced because it is only a thought. When it arrives, it is the present.

There are variations of present moment anchoring practices and you may even discover a version at a later date which serves you but isn't outlined below.

> *I would suggest to invite these practices with open mindness and as outlined previously, be aware of the conditioned mind and the drip of doubt it may commentate whilst you develop your relationship with thinking. Recognise when this happens, it is normal and even to be expected.*

Offer no resistance, acknowledge and return to your practice. The noise of the conditioned mind is not your enemy, it is simply acting out of habit and so it takes some time to develop a new life serving habit.

The mind has been used to your attention for a long time and thus expects your attention. So when you attempt to deny the mind of this, not through aggression, but through diverting your attention, feelings of conflict may arise.

> *Like a gravitational pull the mind will attempt to lure you back, resisting that is where the discomfort arises from.*

It is similar to the smoke alarm sounding in your kitchen. The discomfort is being aware of the noise, but choosing to acknowledge it and return to your practice.

∫∫

> *"Are you out of your mind? Come to your senses!"*

Statements like this are rarely vocalized with any deep sentiment but in a moment of confusion, or poor judgement, the words are of great significance. When you experience a moment of foolishness and you are caught up in thinking it can serve you to step 'out of your mind'. Not literally of course, but to detach from the incessant stream of thinking which is likely clouding your judgement in that moment. As you step out of your mind, you step into your sense perception, or come to your senses, you experience the moment without the noise of the conditioned mind. This is the essence of the present moment.

When you practice these grounding techniques I would advise to do so both in and out of times of suffering. That is, you are not relying on the practices to serve you only in a moment of negative thinking, anxiety and so on. The tools can be explored and developed in times of stillness also.

The inner body

Arrive into the present moment by giving your full attention to the energy of the inner body. This may appear like quite a meditative term, but it can be discovered instantly by anybody. You may wish to read the text below until you become familiar with the essence. You can then practice this yourself.

> *I invite you to close your eyes and hold your hands out in front of you palms open, upwards facing. In your mind I ask you to explore the depth, the thickness, of your palm. Perhaps you could compare it to the depth of a house. There is a top layer, the attic of your palm, and the dorsal side representing the basement. There is immense depth.*

Explore any sensations which you encounter.

With your eyes remaining closed, how do your hands even exist?

You can probably feel 'something'.

What is that feeling? Learn everything you can about it.

It may be tingly, or warm. It has an aliveness.

The feeling which you are experiencing is the energy of your inner body.

When you are fully concentrating on that energy it is not possible to be thinking of anything else. If thought arises in this moment then you are not yet giving your fullest attention to the inner body. In the absence of thought you are grounded in the present moment, with the only sensory input being the energy sensation of the inner body. This is separate from thinking, it is observing or witnessing in a state of alert presence.

Sense perception

The senses (seeing, hearing, touch, taste, smell) will guide you to presence and the tool of sense perception can be incorporated into almost every day to day task. In this state you are giving each moment your fullest attention.

For example, when you wash your hands, you watch the water

flow between your fingers, you smell the scent of the soap, the sound of the water hitting the basin and so on. You are immersed in the moment in its totality. During this moment be free from narrating what you are perceiving. You are aware and alert but without thought.

Your senses are a friend, they bring you the gift of presence. When you divert your attention to your senses they will provide you with a richer life experience.

Taking a conscious breath

Taking a conscious breath can be seen as a mental time out which incorporates the previous two practices. When you become aware of the busyness of the mind, take one, or a few conscious breaths and sense the mental activity dissolve.

Give your breathing it your fullest attention, as you inhale you are feeling the air travelling inside, the expansion of the chest, the exhaled air and so on. This can be repeated as frequently as you like. If your mind interrupts, that is fine, acknowledge and return to the practice.

18

The wilderness years

I considered leaving this chapter out altogether to avoid conflict with the purpose of the book; to open doors within yourself. But perhaps certain points may resonate with your own story and maybe it gives weight to the written words knowing that the author experienced his own awakening journey.

Today I do not identify with those wilderness years as anything other than the years that happened to me. It was a time of my life that would commonly be labelled as 'bad'. On reflection none of it was bad, none of it was good, it simply was.

I'd like to share with you a part of my own story. I too was at the mercy of the conditioned mind but more so I was totally identified with the thoughts I mispercieved as belonging to me.

At this time I was also unaware that I was even identified with thinking. I didn't know such a thing even existed. In hindsight there was some early form of awareness, more so some form of recognition that my mind activity was being troublesome and problematic, but awareness was not developed to the point where it could serve me.

For many years I suffered from, and was often totally debilitated by, my conditioned mind. More so the relationship I held with the mind activity which I experienced.

> *At the time I was under the disillusion that the negative thoughts I experienced were responsible for my unhappiness: but it was the level of credence I gave to the thoughts which was from where the suffering emerged.*

The weight which the identification with thought carried was overwhelming and to myself there was no differentiation between I and thought. They had merged: the thoughts which I had were I and I was my thoughts. This part of my life, the wilderness years, spanned in hostility for 6 years or so. Throughout this time I never encountered thoughts of suicide, though in similar essence my present and future life was seen through a heavy veil of ambiguity.

When I cast my mind back to that time there are specific moments where I felt complete hopelessness and despair. I remember one particular moment in all its lucidity. One night I was inhibited by the most overwhelming anxiety and fear. In a state of panic I remember catching a glimpse of myself in the bathroom mirror, which pulled me in to to stop and stare at the reflection. I focused on my eyes, they were wild, the kind you would expect to see on someone who had encountered a moment which threatened their very existence. In that moment that it is how it felt. In the coming days that image returned to my consciousness and I revisited it with curiosity.

I appeared possessed, almost as if the reflection wasn't me.

Without knowing, this was a profound realisation which was of great significance to my recovery. Though I wasn't aware at the time, my conclusion was quite correct: I was possessed. Not by a demonic figure portrayed in horror films, but possessed by thought. Thought was using me, manifesting in me, and I was its slave. I was imprisoned by my own mind and I was at the mercy of thinking.

The realisation was slow but the awareness grew. There was still continuous noise in my mind but at times it became quiet. Occasionally thinking would transcend from a place of fear to curiosity: I understood that these thoughts which I identified with were happening to me as I could not stop them. I also found myself disagreeing with some of the obsessive thoughts which had taken control of my life. Which led me to this question,

"If the thoughts are happening to me and I don't agree with them, why am I even listening to them?"

I remember one night I was stood on the balcony of my City centre flat, observing the night life. At around midnight I stared down at what was the end of the night for many. In the space of a few minutes I observed people being ejected from bars, fighting in the streets and people vomiting. It was quite chaotic to witness, but I felt an immense feeling of calmness and peace. I was passively watching life but from the perspective of presence, without any judgement or labelling. Though I didn't acknowledge this at the time, I was in a state of alert presence. What made this experience surreal to me was this was during a time when my own mind seemed to be racing from one thought to the next.

It was as if I'd stumbled upon a wormhole which transported me into the eye of the storm. Complete safety, and without thought.

Not long after and the fleeting visit to the eye of the storm dissolved, and the incessant stream of thinking prevailed, but in time this seemingly insignificant moment proved to be of great importance. It was the first moment where I found ultimate peace at a time of ultimate pain. This didn't signal the end of suffering, more so it was the beginning to my awakening journey. There was a growing realisation that I wasn't my thoughts and that the very idea of relating a sense of self to thought was also a great misidentification.

In time I would spend less time thinking, though I wasn't always aware of this improvement as such: in the absence of thought there was no internal narrative to note I wasn't taking part in thinking. But when reflecting on the previous time period, I was able to recognise a changing relationship with thought and how the once incessant stream of thinking had began to dissolve.

For many awakening out of suffering is a process and a journey but for others it can arrive spontaneously, seemingly like a flick of a switch. This occurrence has been spoken of frequently with many experiencing an awakening in the moments before an act of suicide, or when a person cannot stand living any more and they have no option but to give up.

> *In these instances there is an act of desperation, from which the true I surrenders. It no longer fights and instead accepts what is. A suicide does take place, but it is the ego which dies.*

When the mind made imprisonment of ego is surrendered, the attachment to conditioned thinking and all which that represents, also departs.

19

A life of now

We are the only creature on the Earth that is referred to as a being. The basic qualification is that we know how to be.

When you are able to identify the true I, you are no longer searching for identity in fleeting moments. Your values are the cornerstone of you as a person and appeasing values, not the ego, is the key to unlocking a life free from mind made suffering.

Discover more about who you are with curiosity and let values guide you in the actions and thoughts which you make: you are never too young nor old to realise the deeper dimension of the true I.

It has taken time for the conditioning of your mind to become established and so in similar essence the teachings found within this book may also take time to develop. That is not to say they will take years, new habits can manifest in a matter of days to weeks.

The true I will become primary once the noise around you begins to dissolve. It is a journey in which each moment has purpose and so it serves to experience it as such. Time is the energy to which teachings may grow, so new practices should not be rushed.

Patience is needed with a flexible mindset, and of course, the awareness of reluctance from the conditioned mind to invite change.

If you have found yourself resonating with certain points within the book, your own awakening journey to a deeper self and richer life has already begun.

From reading the Little Book of Now to entering a life of now.

Your true self awaits.

Printed in Great Britain
by Amazon